Welcome to "Let Go" - A Coloring Journey to Release and Heal

Life sometimes brings us relationships that start beautifully but, over time, may become difficult or even toxic. Holding onto these relationships can drain our energy, cloud our happiness, and keep us from experiencing the peace we deserve. Letting go of someone who has been an important part of our life is challenging but can ultimately lead us to a stronger, healthier version of ourselves.

What is "Letting Go"?

"Letting go" means releasing attachment to the emotional burdens, pain, and memories that keep us tied to the past. It's not about erasing the relationship from our lives but about freeing ourselves from the negative impact it may have had on us. Letting go allows us to find closure, to forgive ourselves, and to create space for new growth and healthier connections.

The Process of Letting Go

Letting go of a toxic relationship is a personal journey and may look different for everyone, but the general process involves:

1. **Acknowledging Your Feelings**
2. **Focusing on Self-Care**
3. **Releasing Negative Thoughts**
4. **Building a Vision for Your Life:**
5. **Practicing Forgiveness:**

H**ow This Coloring Book Will Help**

"**Let Go Toxic Relationships"- A Coloring Journey to Release and Heal** is 30-pages of coloring book designed to guide you through this journey, on the left page you have reflective question and a note pad to write your thoughts. On the right Page is the let Go quote to encourage and inspire with the Coloring Design. As you color each page, use this time to reflect on the positive message and what it means for you in your healing process. The act of coloring itself can be deeply therapeutic, providing a gentle, creative outlet to release feelings and focus your mind.

Each quote is chosen to help you through stages of release, forgiveness, and renewal, empowering you to embrace the future with hope and clarity. We hope this book becomes a companion on your journey to letting go, helping you find peace, strength, and a renewed sense of self. Remember, letting go isn't a one-time event but a process—and every page you complete is a step closer to healing.

Welcome to the journey. Here's to releasing the past and embracing a brighter future!

Disclaimer

The content in **Let Go of Toxic Relationships: A Therapeutic Coloring Journey to Healing and Renewal** is intended for informational and inspirational purposes only. This book is not a substitute for professional advice, diagnosis, or treatment. If you are experiencing significant emotional distress or mental health concerns, please consult with a qualified healthcare provider, therapist, or counselor.

The exercises, quotes, and reflections in this book are designed to encourage mindfulness, self-expression, and healing but should not be considered a comprehensive treatment plan. Individual results may vary, and readers are encouraged to approach this journey at their own pace.

The author and publisher make no guarantees regarding the outcomes or effectiveness of the practices in this book and disclaim any liability arising from the use or misuse of its contents. If you are under the care of a medical professional or therapist, please consult them before incorporating any new practices into your healing process.

Your well-being is important, and seeking help from trained professionals is a vital part of any healing journey.

Copyrights and Trademarks

Let Go of Toxic Relationships: A Coloring Journey to Release and Heal

.

For permissions, inquiries, or collaboration requests, please contact:

Sudhakar nandury. Email: depthads@gmail.com

Disclaimer: This book is intended for personal reflection and therapeutic purposes. It is not a substitute for professional mental health advice or treatment.

I let go of my relationship with (name)

....

Identify the Toxicity: Think of a specific moment when you realized this relationship was harming you. How did that realization make you feel, and what thoughts came to mind? What did you want for yourself in that moment? Be Mindful with yourself. Just 'Acknowledging Your Feelings & Thoughts.

I choose
peace
over
toxic love.

I let go of my relationship with (name)

Emotional Impact: Reflect on how this relationship has affected your self-esteem. Are there certain words or actions from that time that you still carry with you? How can acknowledging this impact help you let go?

I
deserve peace,
so I'm
letting go.

I let go of my relationship with (name)

....

Boundaries and Needs: Consider a time when your boundaries were crossed in this relationship. How did you respond? What boundaries do you need now to feel safe and valued in future relationships?

I
choose myself
over
this pain.

I let go of my relationship with (name)

....

Rediscovering Your Worth: How did this relationship shape your view of yourself? What qualities do you want to rediscover or reaffirm about yourself as you move forward?

I
release
what doesn't
nurture me.

I let go of my relationship with (name)

....

Letting Go of Guilt: Do you feel any guilt about leaving or ending this relationship? Reflect on why that might be. How can releasing this guilt free you to move toward healing?

Goodbye to
what no
longer serves
me.

I let go of my relationship with (name)

....

Recognizing Red Flags: Looking back, are there warning signs or red flags you wish you'd recognized earlier? Write about what you've learned from these signs and how they can guide you in the future.

I’m
free from
toxic
connections
today.

I let go of my relationship with (name)

....

Embracing New Beginnings: What are you most looking forward to as you let go of this relationship? Describe the kind of peace or freedom you envision for yourself.

I
reclaim
my power ,
starting
now.

I let go of my relationship with (name)

....

A Message to Your Past Self: Imagine you could speak to yourself during the hardest moments of this relationship. What advice or comfort would you give yourself?

I'm
letting go with
love
and grace.

I let go of my relationship with (name)

....

Forgiving Yourself: If you feel regret for any choices you made in the relationship, write about them here. What steps can you take to forgive yourself and accept these as part of your growth?

I
release
myself from
this
weight.

I let go of my relationship with (name)

....

Cultivating Self-Compassion: Write about a time you felt weak or vulnerable in this relationship. How can you offer yourself kindness and compassion for these moments now?

I
deserve love
that heals,
not hurts.

I let go of my relationship with (name)

....

Learning from Loss: How has this experience shaped your understanding of love and partnership? In what ways can these lessons help you build healthier connections moving forward?

I’m leaving
what drains
my spirit.

I let go of my relationship with (name)

....

Recognizing Strengths: Describe a moment when you stood up for yourself or held firm on your boundaries, no matter how small. How did this make you feel? How can you celebrate this strength?

It's time
to protect
my peace

I let go of my relationship with (name)

....

Moving Past Anger: Write about any anger you still feel toward this person. What does this anger tell you about your values and needs? How might releasing this anger help you?

I
let go
for my own
happiness

I let go of my relationship with (name)

....

Reclaiming Your Joy: Reflect on what brings you joy, peace, or excitement outside of relationships. How can you bring more of these activities into your life as you let go?

No more
holding onto
what
harms me

I let go of my relationship with (name)

....

Finding Gratitude: Despite the pain, what are some positive things you learned from this experience? Write down any insights you feel grateful for as you move forward.

I release
the chains
of this
bond

I let go of my relationship with (name)

....

Visualizing Freedom: Close your eyes and imagine a life free from this toxic relationship. What does it look like, and how does it feel? Write down the details of this vision.

Today,
I choose
freedom over
hurt

I let go of my relationship with (name)

....

Setting Intentions for Healing: What intentions would you like to set for your healing journey? How do you want to feel about yourself as you grow beyond this experience?

I deserve
respect,
so I let go

I let go of my relationship with (name)

....

Accepting Change: What changes do you notice in yourself after leaving this relationship? Are there parts of yourself you're still trying to reconnect with or nurture?

I'm
stronger
without this
negativity

I let go of my relationship with (name)

....

Writing a Release Letter: Write a letter to this person expressing anything left unsaid. Share your feelings, frustrations, and what you need to say to fully let go. (Note: you don't have to send it.)

I
let go
to find
my peace

I let go of my relationship with (name)

....

Letting Go of “What Ifs”: Are there any ‘what ifs’ that still linger in your mind about this relationship? Reflect on how releasing these thoughts could help you find closure.

This
chapter ends
for my
growth

I let go of my relationship with (name)

……………………………………

Evaluating Self-Worth: How did this relationship affect the way you see your own worth? List three things that make you worthy of love and respect, just as you are.

I free
myself
from toxic
energy

I let go of my relationship with (name)

....

Finding Closure within Yourself: If closure with the other person isn't possible, what would closure look like if it came only from within? How can you give that to yourself?

I'm
choosing
to heal by
letting go

I let go of my relationship with (name)

....

Exploring Forgiveness (Optional): Do you feel ready to forgive this person, or do you feel it may be part of your healing journey in the future? What would forgiveness mean to you in this context?

No more
hurt;
I'm moving
on

....

Self-Care Affirmations: Write three affirmations that affirm your self-worth and well-being. For example, ‘I deserve respect’ or ‘I choose to heal.’ How do these words make you feel?

I let go
to welcome
healthier
love

I let go of my relationship with (name)

....

Reflecting on Trust: How has this experience affected your ability to trust others? What steps can you take to rebuild trust, starting with yourself?

I deserve
better,
so I'm
releasing this

I let go of my relationship with (name)

....

Honoring Your Journey: What personal qualities helped you through this difficult relationship? How can you honor your resilience as you let go?

I'm
choosing
myself,
finally

I let go of my relationship with (name)

....

Acknowledging Unmet Needs: What needs were unmet in this relationship, and how did that make you feel? Write about how you can meet those needs for yourself moving forward.

I
walk away
to find
my light

I let go of my relationship with (name)

Celebrating Small Wins: Write about one small step you've taken toward letting go, even if it feels minor. Why is this step significant for your growth?

I
let go
for my
future self

I let go of my relationship with (name)

....

Giving Yourself Permission: What do you need to give yourself permission to feel or do in this healing process? How might granting yourself this freedom aid in letting go?

This no
longer fits
my life

I let go of my relationship with (name)

....

Empowering Your Future Self: Imagine yourself one year from now, fully healed and at peace. What would you want to tell your current self as encouragement on this journey?

I choose
peace over
toxic love

www.ingramcontent.com/pod-product-compliance
Lightning Source LLC
LaVergne TN
LVHW070943160826
845679LV00022B/1895
9798896730453